I bfaiteadh na súl · I ndorċadas an lae
bruiġ do béal ġo tobann ar mo béalsa ·
Aġus sloġadh mé ġo ġlan i ġclapsholas
domain do póige ~

I bfaiteadh na mbéal · I bfriotal na súl
fásaidh aġus teannadh · ġo dtí naċ raib ann
Aċ scáṫ an scannáin eadrann, ċoiṫ
I do ċluais istiġ ~

Mé i mo ċost anois, dlaoiċe ċasta do ṫairte
ina luí ġo dlúṫ ar urlár snasta, mé á
scuabadh, mé á scaipeadh, séideán beaġ
amuiġ ~

do Deirdre,   Ciaranus Carsoni fecit

béal feirste   A·D· 1994

a dark umbrella
passing ~ only one, where it
is snowing. nightfall

D0602683

Ciaran Carson : FIRST LANGUAGE : *Poems*

Ciaran Carson
First Language
Poems

Wake Forest University Press

Published in North America by Wake Forest University Press in 1994. Text designed by Peter Fallon and published in Ireland and the United Kingdom by Gallery Press. Copyright © Ciaran Carson 1994. All rights reserved. For permission, required to reprint or broadcast more than several lines, write to Wake Forest University Press, Winston-Salem, NC 27109.
ISBN 0–916390–61–6 (cloth); ISBN 0–916390–60–8 (paper).
Library of Congress Card Number 94–60031.

Contents

for Deirdre

La Je-Ne-Sais-Quoi

I bhfaiteadh na súl
I ndorchadas an lae
Bhrúigh do bhéal go tobann
Ar mo bhéalsa
Agus slogadh mé go glan
I gclapsholas domhain do phóige.

I bhfaiteadh na mbéal
I bhfriotal na súl
Fáscadh agus teannadh
Go dtí nach raibh ann
Ach scáth an scátháin eadrainn,
Tocht i do chluais istigh.

Mé i mo thost anois,
Dlaoithe chasta do chainte
Ina luí go dlúth ar urlár snasta,
Mé á scuabadh, mé á scaipeadh
Go béal an dorais,
Séideán beag amuigh.

Second Language

English not being yet a language, I wrapped my lubber-lips
    around my thumb;
Brain-deaf as an embryo, I was snuggled in my comfort-
    blanket dumb.

Growling figures campaniled above me, and twanged their
    carillons of bronze
Sienna consonants embedded with the vowels *alexandrite*,
    emerald and *topaz*.

The topos of their discourse seemed to do with me and
    convoluted genealogy;
Wordy whorls and braids and skeins and spiral helices,
    unskeletoned from laminate geology —

How this one's slate-blue gaze is correspondent to
    another's new-born eyes;
Gentians, forget-me-nots, and cornflowers, diurnal in a
    heliotrope surmise.

Alexandrine tropes came gowling out like beagles, loped and
    unroped
On a snuffly Autumn. Nimrod followed after with his bold
    Arapahoes,

Who whooped and hollered in their unforked tongue. The trail
    was starred with
Myrrh and frankincense of Anno Domini; the Wise Men
    wisely paid their tariff.

A single star blazed at my window. Crepuscular, its acoustic
    perfume dims
And swells like flowers on the stanzaic-papered wall.
    Shipyard hymns

Then echoed from the East: gantry-clank and rivet-ranks, Six-
    County hexametric
Brackets, bulkheads, girders, beams, and stanchions;
    convocated and Titanic.

Leviathans of rope snarled out from ropeworks: disgorged
    hawsers, unkinkable lay,
Ratlines, S-twists, plaited halyards, Z-twists, catlines; all had
    their say.

Tobacco-scent and snuff breathed out in gouts of factory
    smoke like aromatic camomile;
Sheaves of brick-built mill-stacks glowered in the sulphur-
    mustard fog like campaniles.

The dim bronze noise of midnight-noon and Angelus then
    boomed and clinked in Latin
Conjugations; statues wore their shrouds of amaranth; the
    thurible chinked out its smoky patina.

I inhaled *amo, amas, amat* in quids of *pros* and *versus* and
    Introibos
Ad altare Dei; incomprehensibly to others, spoke in Irish. I
    slept through the Introit.

The enormous Monastery surrounded me with nave and
    architrave. Its ornate pulpit
Spoke to me in fleurs-de-lys of Purgatory. Its sacerdotal gaze
    became my pupil.

My pupil's nose was bathed in Pharaonic unguents of dope and
    glue.
Flimsy tissue-paper plans of aeroplanes unfolded whimsical
    ideas of the blue,

Where, unwound, the prop's elastic is unpropped and balsa-
   wood extends its wings
Into the hazardous azure of April. It whirrs into the realm of
   things.

Things are kinks that came in tubes; like glue or paint
   extruded, that became
A hieroglyphic alphabet. Incestuous in pyramids, Egyptians
   were becalmed.

I climbed into it, delved its passageways, its sepulchral
   interior, its things of kings
Embalmed; sarcophagi, whose perfume I exhumed in chancy
   versions of the *I-Ching*.

A chink of dawn was revelated by the window. Far-off cocks
   crowed crowingly
And I woke up, verbed and tensed with speaking English; I
   lisped the words so knowingly.

I love the as-yet morning, when no one's abroad, and I am like
   a postman on his walk,
Distributing strange messages and bills, and arbitrations with
   the world of talk:

I foot the snow and almost-dark. My shoes are crisp, and bite
   into the blue-
White firmament of pavement. My father holds my hand and
   goes blah-

Blah with me into the ceremonial dawn. I'm wearing tweed.
   The universe is Lent
And Easter is an unspun cerement, the gritty, knitty, tickly
   cloth of unspent

Time. I feel its warp and weft. Bobbins pirn and shuttle in
    Imperial
Typewriterspeak. I hit the keys. The ribbon-black clunks out
    the words in serial.

What comes next is next, and no one knows the *che sera* of it,
    but must allow
The *Tipp-Ex* present at the fingertips. Listen now: an angel
    whispers of the here-and-now.

The future looms into the mouth incessantly, gulped-at and
    unspoken;
Its guardian is intangible, but gives you hints and winks and
    nudges as its broken token.

I woke up blabbering and dumb with too much sleep. I rubbed
    my eyes and ears.
I closed my eyes again and flittingly, forgetfully, I glimpsed
    the noise of years.

A Date Called *Eat Me*

The American Fruit Company had genetically engineered a
    new variety of designer apple,
Nameless as yet, which explored the various Platonic ideals of
    the 'apple' synapse.

Outside the greengrocer's lighted awning it is dusky
    Hallowe'en. It is
Snowing on a box of green apples, crinkly falling on the tissue
    paper. It is

Melting on the green, unbitten, glistening apples, attracted by
    their gravity.
I yawned my teeth and bit into the dark, mnemonic cavity.

That apple-box was my first book-case. I covered it in wood-
    grain *Fablon* —
You know that Sixties stick-on plastic stuff? I thought it
    looked dead-on:

Blue Pelicans and orange Penguins, *The Pocket Oxford
    English Dictionary*;
Holmes and Poe, *The Universe*, the fading aura of an apple
    named *Discovery* —

I tried to extricate its itsy-bitsy tick of rind between one tooth
    and another tooth,
The way you try to winkle out the 'facts' between one truth
    and another truth.

Try to imagine the apple talking to you, tempting you like
    something out of Aesop,
Clenched about its navel like a fist or face, all pith and pips and
    sap

Or millions of them, hailing from the heavens, going *pom,*
  pom, pom, pom, pom
On the roof of the American Fruit Company, whose computer
  banks are going *ohm* and *om*.

They were trying to get down to the nitty-gritty, sixty-four-
  thousand dollar question of whether the stalk
Is apple or branch or what. The programme was stuck.

The juice of it explodes against the roof and tongue, the cheek
  of it.
I lied about the *Fablon,* by the way. It was really midnight
  black with stars on it.

Grass

We'd done a deal of blow, and dealt a hand or two of Brag,
Which bit by bit became a bloody Patience, except no one
Seemed to twig which hand was which, or who was who or
    whom
Or what was ace or deuce.

Hardly any shock, when in the general boggledybotch, the
    budgie
Unlatched himself from out the room, and what he cheeped
    and Canterburied
Wasn't Gospel — which hardly gave a fiddler's, since the flats
    were on the bias
Or on the juice.

It was the circumbendibus of everything that got us locked
And scuttered, the Anno Domini of what had happened
    yonks before
Our time, and that is why we languish now in Anguagela Jail,
    while he
Is on the loose.

For what the blatherskite had shit was mouth a bow-wow
Word or two and let the echolalia hang out — which the
    Powers-that-Be
Lapped up, since they never liked to Brian O'Lynn the sup
    without
Its inkling of Vermouth.

What we had on us would do and, if not, they'd make it more,
The way an ounce of dope becomes a key. They took it down
    in notes
Contemporaneously, and the brief told us to sing our prayers,
    but not the sort the boys
Learn in Maynooth.

My curse upon this few-cards-missing-from-the-deck who
    lately soldiered o'er
From Cant; Archbishoply he took us in. But his crinkum-
    crankum ways
Will lead him to Brazil, if that is what he thinks he is as hard as;
He'll do his bird in Braggadocia and learn the truth.

Two to Tango

Whether you want to change your face or not's up to yourself.
    But the bunk of history
They'll make up for you. Someone else's shoes. They can put
    you anywhere. Where's a mystery.

Aromas, sounds, the texture of the roads, the heaviness or
    lightness of the air —
All these contribute to the sense of place. These things are what
    we are,

Though mitigated by ourselves. The details might be
    anywhere, so long as a romantic atmosphere
Is evoked. But to mention Africa, the Middle East or Russia is
    anathema.

It's not the money. Money enters into it, but doesn't talk. I do
    that.
I fill the blanks they know already. I'm the jammy centre in the
    doughnut.

Introspection must serve a purpose beyond the simple passing
    of time:
That bit of dialogue, recalled, might prove to be the clue that
    solves the crime.

And Belfast isn't like Beirut, although I've never been there.
    It's what it is:
Agendas, bricks and mortar, interfaces. Others in the structure
    like me. *Veritas*.

Dialogue can act as a transition bridge: for example, *I've been
    meaning to talk to you,*
He said, *I hear you've got the job . . . that you'll have to move
    to Tokyo . . .*

They can't let on I'm there. There's nothing down on paper.
  What there is is code.
Alone? I'm sometimes. Very. Very. Sometimes very hot and
  sometimes very cold.

*She watched the way the hair on his wrist curled round the
  band of his wrist-watch:*
This is an example of 'initial entanglement', from which it's
  difficult to wrench

Herself. Others might be fragrances, like melted candle-wax; .
  sometimes, even, sweat.
And the timepiece might be Philippe Patek, but never, under
  any circumstances, *Swatch*.

You find ways around it, yawning, getting up to 'go out for a
  couple of hours'.
They make the place secure for you. It's like a Twilight Zone
  where they exert their Special Powers.

And you make sure you don't repeat yourself. Change the
  routine ever
So slightly. Tell no one, I mean no one, what you're up to.
  Never. Never. Never.

Use slang and buzz-words sparingly. Use body language tags,
  especially for men:
*He punctuated his words with repeated clicks of his Mont Blanc
  ball-point pen.*

For when you stop saying *never*, that's when you'll get dead.
  You'll put your sweet lips
A little too close to the phone and talk of *always* in a fatal
  momentary lapse.

And then you think, not to repeat yourself is not real life. And
    so you do.
You develop mannerisms. Tics and tags, without them looking
    like they're pseudo.

And contrast is important, between male and female dialogue.
    Then there's changes of identity;
But be careful of the cliché where the protagonist is torn
    between identical

Twins. A hero, me? I'm not. It's just a game. I'm saving lives?
    Perhaps.
It's like a sentence crammed with grammar, phrases, ages,
    hyphens, stops.

Is this a faction or a *roman fleuve* (more commonly called
    generational
Or *saga*)? Decide before you start, work out your plot, then go
    for it. *Be inspirational.*

One side says this, the other that. You work it out yourself and
    walk between the story lines.
What's true is what you do. Keep your head down. Know
    yourself. Ignore the starry skies.

Ovid: *Metamorphoses*, V, 529-550

Persephone ate seven pomegranate seeds. So what? I'll tell you
    what —
It doesn't do to touch strange fruit, when it's forbidden by the
    Powers-
That-Be. Who put you on a hunger strike which, if you break,
    you'll stay put
In the Underworld. It doesn't do to get caught out. Watch
    out for prowlers.

She'd wandered into Pluto's murky realm; plucked the dull-
    orange bubble.
Split the cortex. Sucked. And who was salivating in the bushes'
    dark interior
But Ascalaphus. Stoolie. Pipsqueak. Mouth. He spilled the
    beans on her, he blabbed —
Straight off he shot, and knocked, knocked, knocked on
    Heaven's iron door.

But she spat back as good as she had got: unholy water from
    the Phlegethon
She slabbered on him. His eyes yellowed, drooled, and grew.
    His neb became a beak.
He sprouted spermy wings. Hooked talons shot from his
    fingers. His body dwindled
Into mostly head. All ears, all eyes: touts everywhere,
    potential freaks,

Beware. For now he is the scrake-owl, Troubles' augury for
    Auld Lang Syne,
Who to this day is harbinger of doom, the gloom of Pluto's
    no-go zone.

Four Sonnets

1

The crushed carapaces of watches ticked on the pavement. Passers-by ignored them.

Put your ear to the street, you will hear the underground streams of Belfast.

'The bodies that clothe them are enfeebled,' said the Dalai Lama momentarily.

The seagulls' white *ms* skittered and mewed behind the noisy Doppler-red fire engines.

But it is business as usual and there is already new glass to be stared through.

All over the city, the stopped clocks told each other the different wrong times.

The black electric flex snaked through the air-vent to remind you of a bug.

'Planting through the new man-made membrane can be a bit fiddly.'

With his fingernail and quick, he unlatched the little crucifix's coffin-lid.

'This morning's lesson is "psychotherapeutic evaluation". Multiple choices are allowed.'

Don't ever sit around in your costume. Don't *ever* put your puppet face-down.

'*Not* business solutions.' 'But there are so many lookalikes.'
'Wrong again.'

I lost the key to the refreshment centre. Babies. Splits. *Cidona*.
Squash. Dash.

He breathed Gethsemane. They began to search the labyrinth
of the thumb-print.

2

He splashed Polish spirit on his wrist, set fire to it, and didn't
burn.

Tomorrow? That's the Twelfth of Nevuary, man — like, Oh,
Zero, Nought, Nix.

One of the puppets is 'The Disjointed Policeman'. Then
there's Punch. They share the truncheon.

There *are* so many lookalikes. The way you know the black
boxer by his white shorts.

It was printed on *Weetabix* paper with some dense black ink by
a former Soviet.

He did his chicken-with-the-head-cut-off walk, then
staggered out. No strings attached.

I examined the calamine-lotion-pink of the tax form till I was
tired.

'The South Georgian onions had a bad Spring, so Anton
decided to use the Spanish instead.'

The cidermen were in direct contravention of an alcohol-free zone.

'Everybody cries. Some like you did. Some inside. What you did's better.'

In the Conrad Hotel the delegates walked round pretending not to read their name-tags.

There's a space the thickness of rice-paper between your feet and the stage.

'It's a non-consumptive, non-polluting industry,' said the injection apparatus operator.

The legs hang from the shoulder. The heads are kept separate from the bodies.

3

The white security tape has been taken away, but I wouldn't go out, if I were you.

After I changed the ribbon I realised everything was finger-printed.

The deaf-mute held a lemon in his hand for want of a better word.

'Well, one day the statue was there, and the next it wasn't.'

When the innocent was released he was speedily embraced by Special Powers.

Why the shattered window, when the door's unlatched and
   creaking?

It's the aerosol 'pine' aroma that goes with the log-effect
   electric fire.

The holes were drilled in the scales of Justice to let out the
   rainwater.

Like the man says, 'You don't have to know how a thing
   works to know it *isnae* working.'

Summer lightning: the blackthorn hedge wavered like a foot
   patrol.

He had his two arms full of analogue and digital, Arabic and
   Roman watchstraps.

I opened the fridge; a blast of cold air slapped me in the face
   like light.

'He's trying to play the crocodile — and what is he? He's the
   lizard under the rock.'

I was trying to tell the time when I swallowed a lemon pip from
   my sixth or seventh gin-and-tonic.

   4

Who is the leader? What is the gang? Give me the initials of the
   gang!

'Magenta' summoned up the battle of Magenta.

'Prisoners on the roof are dismantling the roof in a desperate
  bid for freedom.'

I spilled the milk. A little, dog-eared map of Ireland
  sprawled on the Axminster.

He was full as a goog or a sheugh. Legless. Half-cut. Half-lit.
  Getting there.

In February the ice-cream chimes played *The Teddy-Bears'
  Picnic*.

The sniffer dog wriggled its way into focus the way it waggled
  its tail.

They were attached to each other in the loops of
  Messerschmidt and Hurricane.

First the bare notes. Then staccato. Then the off-beat.
  Counterpoint. *Stop*. You forgot the soul.

The tickly corrugations of the *Tintawn* that he barefoot crept
  downstairs upon.

You mistook the Californian oranges for Seville. One is
  bumpier.

It was the way he noticed the man who was playing the saw had
  only a leg.

Be Born Again! Be Saved! Wash yourself in the Blood of the
  Lamb!

On Not Remembering Some Lines of a Song

It's the pawl-and-ratchet mechanism
Of one of those antique, whirligig-type, wooden rattles, only
Some of the teeth are missing. Or there's fluff
On the needle of the pick-up, and bursts of steam —
Ampersands, asterisks, and glottal stops — puff round
The words, like those signals in the distance
That announce the almost-imminent arrival
Of the train which everyone had given up for lost.

If I'd been you, I wouldn't have started
Off from here, the anxious tourist was informed. He'd come
Prepared for rain, but dusk was streaming
Down on the little station, on
His orange oilskins. Over and above the musk
Of creosote and hawthorn, he could just make out
The pipe bands struggling homewards, the skirts
Of clouds obscured by twilit music.

That windblown, martial girn and drone reminded me
I came from the wrong side of the tracks.
The criss-cross meaning of their Black Watch tartan
Was a mystery to me, and I could never fathom
How they synchronized
The swing of their hips, kilts waving like a regiment
Of window-wipers, so the drizzle doesn't fog
Their automatic pilot.

It's coming back in dribs and drabs, for nothing ever
Is forgotten: it's in there somewhere in the memory-bank,
Glimmering in binary notation. I think you have to find
That switch between the *off* and *on*, the split chink
Through which you peer with half an eye
And glimpse the other, time-drenched world.
A jitter of fragmented bird-song, in which the microtones
Are birds, twittering between the staves.

And the demarcation lines of white tape
Drifted into side-streets, tangled up with children's skipping-
Ropes, the hide-and-seek of counting-rhymes.
Evening draws in like a hyphen: the parade
Had ended hours ago
And the Sabbath quiet of that Monday
Had been long implicit in the festival agenda
As the marchers learned to walk again by rote.

The regalia were consigned to the future blue
Where a fancy skywriter lets the message bloom and fluff
And then dissolve before our eyes
Until everything is indecipherable, the blown wisps
Of letters becoming an 'acoustic perfume'. And
The slogan was so perfect, so much
In tune with television jingles, that it seemed to breathe
From everybody's mouths

As if freshly minted there, this squeezed-out root of
    toothpaste
That bears the tang of aromatic speech. It oozes
From the floodlit shrubbery
Where gypsy moths are whirling in commemorative World
    War I
Camouflage, describing Celtic dogfights, loop-
The-loops and tangents. For everything blooms out of
    season:
Surely the children had anticipated all of this, these frosty
    nights;
They counted out the gabbled alphabet of stars.

Apparat

Unparalysed, the robot bomb-disposal expert inched and
tacked across the mezzanine
As casually as someone to be barbered sits relaxing with a
magazine.

It was using 'deep creep' and 'infinite hair', conversing in its
base-of-two conundrum.
Its chips were bugged like all the toasters in the apparatchniks'
condominium.

Turnbull twiddled with the radio controls. He twitched his
robot's claws.
He felt the Mobile Ordinance Disposal Unit index through its
dictionary of clues.

Umbilical, he was in the waiting room. Barberlike, he opened
up his case of instruments.
He was beckoned by the realms of Nod. He entered in with
incense and Byzantine vestments.

The smart bomb got the message and intoned the right
liturgical analysis.
Latinate, they swapped explosive bits and pieces; they re-
emerged in Nemesis.

The Brain of Edward Carson

They cracked the skull and watched its two halves creak
    apart, like the decks
Of some Byzantine trireme. The herringboned, zipped oars,
    the chains and shackles.
The bronze circuitry. The locks. The Titanic, legal depositions
    of the cells.
The hammered rivets. The rivetted, internal gaze. The screws.
    The nails.
The caulked bulwarks. The slaves, embalmed in honeycomb
    prismatic.

Barbaric instruments inserted there, like hook and razor, iron
    picks
By which they will extrapolate its history: the bronze, eternal
    static
Of his right, uplifted hand. The left hand like a shield. The
    bolted-on, external
Eyes. The seraphic frown. The borders and the chains
    contained therein. The fraternal
Gaze of the Exclusive Brethren: orange and bruised purple,
    cataleptic.

The map of Ulster opened up, hexagonal and intricate,
    tectonic:
Its shifting plates were clunked and welded into place by laws
    Masonic.
The ladder and the rope. The codicils. The compasses by
    which they sail
Uncharted futures. The outstretched hand. The crown. The
    sash. The secret nail.
And then disintegration intervened, the brain eluded them:
    Sphinxlike, catatonic.

Opus 14

Hole Blown in Baroque Splendour of Opera House (designed
    by Frank Matcham):
The Security Forces were specifically looking for terrorists but
    spectacularly failed to catch them.

Newly-appointed innumerate Chancellor of the Exchequer
    What-Do-You-Call-Him Clarke
Was counting his stars in twos like the innumerable animals in
    Noah's Ark.

Did you know that 'the set of all objects describable in exactly
    eleven English words'
Is called an 'R-Set'? I didn't. It was dreamed up by the people
    who put the 'surd' in 'absurd'.

Spokesman for censored political party spoke in someone
    else's lip-synch
So perfectly, you'd think it was the man himself, though much
    of this is double-think.

So I woke up this morning with yet another wrong solution to
    Fermat's Last
Theorem, which bore about the same relationship to global x
    as does the world to Atlas.

He had a pocketful of pocket calculators, palindromes, and
    anagrams. The Name
Of Names eluded him as yet, but he was working on it and had
    found the Name of the Game.

The idea was that one and one made three, like in the Holy
    Family
Or Trinity, where 'three' is pronounced 'tree', as in the Irish
    Christian Brother's homily.

I think this goes to show that Cajori's study of mathematical
    symbols
Is in part, like not to see the wood for trees, a graveyard for
    dead symbols.

For you can deconstruct all sorts of words from 'England':
    angel, *gland* and *dangle*;
It's the way the Germans have captured the Gaolainn-speaking
    industry in Dingle.

Sums are funny. *Wars 2. Legs 1. Wives 2. Children 4. Wounds
    2. Total 11.* You know?
Which reminds me to go and check out Nik Cohn's book *Yes,
    We Have No.*

Bananas is understood. It's not known by many, or maybe it
    is, that Cohn's from Londonderry or Derry,
Which might account for the ambivalence of the fact of the
    Foyle's not having a ferry.

Of course, it has this double-decker bridge, at which you're
    doubly checked.
The soldier looks at you and then he looks at your picture. It's
    pronounced *echt*.

At the previous Chancellor's Last Supper, he was seized by a
    sudden triskaidecaphobia
Which took him to the fourteenth floor, where he became
    immersed in a conference of bankers from the Bank of
    Wachovia.

It likes to do that. *Wachovia*. Which brings me back to
    baroque Opera House designed by Frank.
The googolplex security net had been full of innumerable holes
    held together by string, to be frank.

Drunk Boat

After Rimbaud, Le Bateau Ivre

As I glided down the lazy Meuse, I felt my punters had gone
    AWOL —
In fact, Arapahoes had captured them for target practice,
    nailing them to stakes. Oh hell,

I didn't give a damn. I didn't want a crew, nor loads of Belgian
    wheat, nor English cotton.
When the whoops and hollers died away, their jobs were well
    forgotten.

Through the tug and zip of tides, more brain-deaf than an
    embryo, I bobbled;
Peninsulas, unmoored and islanded, were envious of my
    Babel-babble.

Storms presided at my maritime awakening. Like a cork I
    waltzed across the waves,
Which some call sailors' graveyards; but I despised their
    far-off, lighted enclaves.

As children think sour apples to be sweet, so the green sap
    swamped the planks
And washed away the rotgut and the puke, the rudder and the
    anchor-hanks.

I've been immersed, since then, in Sea Poetry, anthologized by
    stars,
As through the greenish Milky Way a corpse drifts down-
    wards, clutching a corrupted spar;

When suddenly, those sapphire blues are purpled by Love's
  rusty red. No lyric
Alcohol, no Harp, can combat it, this slowly-pulsing, twilit
  panegyric.

I've known lightning, spouts, and undertows, maelstrom
  evenings that merge into Aurora's
Blossoming of doves. I've seen the Real Thing; others only get
  its aura.

I've seen the sun's demise, where seas unroll like violet,
  antique
Venetian blinds; dim spotlight, slatted by the backstage work
  of Ancient Greeks.

I dreamed the green, snow-dazzled night had risen up to kiss
  the seas'
Blue-yellow gaze, the million plankton eyes of phosphor-
  escent argosies.

I followed then, for many months, the mad-cow waves of the
  Antipodes,
Oblivious to the Gospel of how Jesus calmed the waters,
  walking on his tippy-toes.

I bumped, you know, into the Floridas, incredible with
  pupil-flowers
And manatees, which panther-men had reined with rainbows
  and with Special Powers.

I saw a whole Leviathan rot slowly in the seething marsh, till
  it became
All grot and whalebone. Blind cataracts lurched into
  oubliettes, and were becalmed.

Glaciers and argent seas, pearly waves and firecoal skies! A
tangled serpent-cordage
Hauled up from the Gulf, all black-perfumed and slabbered
with a monster's verbiage!

I would have liked the children to have seen them: goldfish,
singing-fish, John Dorys —
My unanchored ones, I'm cradled by the tidal flowers and
lifted near to Paradise.

Sometimes, fed-up with the Poles and Zones, the sea would
give a briny sob and ease
Off me; show me, then, her vented shadow-flowers, and I'd be
like a woman on her knees . . . .

Peninsular, I juggled on my decks with mocking-birds and
ostriches
And rambled on, until my frail lines caught another upside-
down, a drowned Australian.

Now see me, snarled-up in the reefs of bladder-wrack, or
thrown by the waterspout like craps
Into the birdless Æther, where Royal Navy men would slag
my sea-drunk corpse —

Smoking, languorous in foggy violet, I breathed a fireglow
patch into
The sky, whose azure trails of snot are snaffled by some Poets
as an entrée —

Electromagnets, hoof-shaped and dynamic, drove the
Nautilus. Black hippocampuses
Escorted it, while heat-waves drummed and blattered on the
July campuses.

Me, I shivered: fifty leagues away, I heard the bumbling
    Behemoths and Scarabs;
Spider spinning in the emerald, I've drifted off the ancient
    parapets of Europe!

Sidereal archipelagoes I saw! Island skies, who madly
    welcomed the explorer;
O million starry birds, are these the endless nights you dream
    of for the Future?

I've whinged enough. Every dawn is desperate, every bitter
    sun. The moon's atrocious.
Let the keel split now, let me go down! For I am bloated, and
    the boat is stotious.

Had I some European water, it would be that cold, black
    puddle
Where a child once launched a paper boat — frail butterfly —
    into the dusk; and huddled

There, I am no more. O waves, you've bathed and cradled me
    and shaped
Me. I'll gaze no more at Blue Ensigns, nor merchantmen, nor
    the drawn blinds of prison-ships.

Second Nature

After Seán Ó Ríordáin, Malairt

'Come over here,' says Turnbull, 'till you see the sorrow in the
　　horse's eyes;
If you had hooves as cumbersome, there would be gloom in
　　your eyes too.'

And it was clear to me, that he had understood the sorrow
　　in the horse's eyes
So well, had dwelt so long on it, that he was plunged in the
　　horse's mind.

I looked over at the horse, that I might see the sorrow pouring
　　from its eyes;
I saw the eyes of Turnbull, looming towards me from the
　　horse's head.

I looked at Turnbull; I looked at him again, and saw beneath
　　his brows
The too-big eyes that were dumb with sorrow, the horse's
　　eyes.

Correspondances

After Baudelaire, Correspondances

Nature is a Temple: its colonnaded trunks blurt out, from time
    to time, a verdurous babble;
The dark symbolic forest eyes you with familiarity, from the
    verge of Parable.

Self-confounding echoes buzz and mingle through the gloomy
    arbours;
Vowels, perfumes, stars swarm in like fireflies from the
    midnight blue of harbours.

The quartet yawns and growls at you with amber, rosin,
    incense, musk;
Horsehair on the catgut is ecstatic with its soul and spirit
    music —

Prairie greens, the *oms* and *ahs* of oboes, soft as the bloom on
    infant
Baby-skin; and other great hits, smothered in the triumph of
    the infinite.

All Souls

The un*Walkman* headphones stick out awkwardly, because
    they are receiving
Not the packaged record of a song, but real-time input, a form
    of blah
Alive with intimations of mortality, the loud and unclear
    garbled static.

It's the peripatetic buzz of static, like it was a Hallowe'enlike
    weather
That you rarely get at Hallowe'en. The mushrooms
    mushroomed as per
Usual, that is to say, in subterfuge, slowly dawning through on
    Instamatic.

Like putting on spectacles, when what it was was blurred, then
    swims
Into your focus. You can see they come from the Planet *X*,
    with their walkie-
Talkies, the heavy warbling of their heavy Heaney tyres and
    automatic,

Gyroscope-type-tank-surveillance technique, their faces
    blacked like
Boots. Their antennae quivered on that Hallowe'en
    encountered just beyond Sans
Souci. It was, in fact, outside the Fire Station, and the firemen,
    with Platonic

Abandon, were going through their exercises, rehearsing for
    the Fire,
The Bomb, the Incident, some routine dot on the dial, where
    the wireless
Lights with intimations of Hilversum or Moscow, and the
    Radio Symphonic

Orchestra is playing someone's Dead March through the
    whistles and the static
Of the dark you listen to. To which you listen, like routine
    intimations
Of the precinct where the oblique Mandarins decreed antique

Examinations. Then the sound was turned up suddenly,
    anorectic candidates
Blew their fuses; they had failed to comprehend their
    hierophantic elders, who
Laid the rubric down so many yonks ago in ancient mnemonic.

Demonic intimations went on daily; routine, undercover
    orchestrations
Of the nominated discipline of alphabetic, proscribed areas
That ended, as they always do, in tragic, tired recriminations;
    rhetoric.

It then occurred the Firemen had a Ball, it was at Hallowe'en.
    Ecstatically, they
Didn't have false faces on. They were plastic, not explosively,
    but faces. Then
They tore their faces off. Un*Walkman*like. Laconic.
    Workmanlike.

From the Welsh

Mountain snow, my drift is deep and thick; the sheep are
    walking on the rooftops.

Mountain snow, the milk is icy; I skim it off to get down to the
    bottom of it.

Mountain snow, the fences under snow; without them, who
    will know his neighbour?

Mountain snow, I climbed it yesterday; eventually, my head
    came through the clouds.

Mountain snow, the eggs are fragile; numbed fingers cannot
    handle them.

Mountain snow, the ducks are out of water; they slither out of
    kilter on the ice.

Mountain snow, the preacher shuts his Bible; his words are
    swallowed in the dark.

Mountain snow, the moorcock crows; his loneliness betrays
    him to the hunter.

Mountain snow, the English are at odds with one another;
    some of them are learning Welsh.

Mountain snow, no light to read a book by; heads are buried
    under bedclothes.

Mountain snow, one eye squeezed against the cold, the hunter
    is a Cyclops.

Mountain snow, a sheep is sprawling in the ditch; one by one,
    the flock falls in with her.

Mountain snow, if words related what the mind knew, none
would be neighbours.

Mountain snow, and there is brawling in the tavern; it is
probably the Irish.

Sonnet

As usual the little container of artificial milk spurted driblets
    on my wrist.

The baby's furled and unfurled fists described the way it
    bawled with its mouth.

'Welcome to Belfast, home of the best knee surgeons in the
    world.'

She fried the fish fingers in cod-liver oil.

'Extra Mild? They'd be no good to me. I'd have to break off the
    cork.'

I so admired the lip-print on the calling-card of the diminutive
    Japanese 'hostess'.

'Let me know the details, including Designer, Printer, and the
    length of run including variables.'

I knew he was a smoker because of the wrinkled eyes. The
    pursed mouth.

Muldoon clutched the wheel of a convertible Hillman Imp
    with the canopy rolled back.

There was a wild rumour that the live band had been lip-
    synched by a rival organisation.

'I apologize if I did not sign the letter that accompanied the
    interview. If I did, forget this note.'

I knew he couldn't be a gardener because of the hours he spent
    with seed catalogues.

The bicycle shop exploded in a shower of cleats, straps,
   sprockets, spindles, cranks, ratchets, levers.

Not to mention the yellow fingers. I prefer the semi-skimmed
   myself.

Ovid: *Metamorphoses*, XIII, 439-575

They'd anchored off the coast of Thrace, Agamemnon and
    the comrades, waiting
For a calm; when suddenly, Achilles' ghost appears from
    nowhere, looking large
As life and twice as natural. Blood-shot glinting in his eye, he
    says,
'Forgetful of me, are you? Think my fame was buried with
    me? No, you'll have to pay
Your dues. Take you Polyxena, and put her through the usual
    rites of sacrifice. Her blood
Will be the mark of your respect.' The comrades looked at one
    another, and in that look
Became blood brothers. They dragged Polyxena from
    Hecuba, her mother.

They bring her to the altar. With sword unscabbarded, the
    priest is waiting.
Then, 'Take off your hands from me,' she says, and rips her
    bodice. Shows
Her throat. Her breast. 'I'll go as someone free. It's not my
    death that grieves me,
But my mother's life. And when she comes to claim my body,
    give it to her
Freely. Don't ask for gold as ransom for this corpse. Exchange
    it for her tears.'
And then she's stabbed and stabbed again, and still her last gasp
    shows no sign of fear.
The Trojan women keened her then, and all the other dead
    ones in the house of Hecuba and Priam.

Here's Hecuba: she stuck her lips to the flapping lips of the
    wound and sucked the blood.
Her hair was slabbered and bedraggled with it. Her salt tears
    watered it.

She clawed and scrabbed herself. Then, 'Daughter, last of all
   my pain, for what
Remains? — I stare into your wound and see my wound, my
   children slaughtered.
Achilles did your brothers in, and you, and emptied me. His
   very ghost
Abuses me. I who was queen. I was someone. Look at me. I'm
   nothing now. I spin my wool
As conversation-piece for that Penelope, who sniggers, "*That*
   was Hector's mother. *That* was Priam's wife."

'And can I be alive? How can I be? O Gods, have you reserved
   some more for me?
New funerals? New death? And who would think that Priam
   would be
Happy? Happy man is he in being dead. And will my daughter
   have a gorgeous funeral?
Pomp and ceremony? Not she. She's planted in this foreign
   heap of sand.
No, wait, no, stay — there's more. There's still my lovely imp,
My little Polydorus. He's alive. He'll keep me. Look after me.
   What *am* I at? I haven't washed
Her wound yet. Her bloodied face. Her wound. I'll get some
   water from the shore.'

Salt water: when she got there, what was there? She shut her
   eyes. She howled.
For what was there was Polydorus, dead. His wounds stared at
   her. The eyes of
The wounds. Their sockets. The emptiness of wounds. She
   petrified herself.
Her stony eyes grazed the ground. The sky. The ground again.
   The sky. And then
She opened sight itself and looked at him. His face. His eyes.
   His hands. His feet. All over.

And then it struck her. Polymestor. King of Thrace. He had to
    be behind it.
Polymester. I'll show him who was queen. Who is. I am. I'll
    be. I'll get him yet.

She's like a lioness, robbed of her cubs, who crouches, shivers,
    creeps in for the kill.
She howled again. Shook her bedraggled hair. Set out for him,
    and gained an interview.
Said she had some gold, she'd kept for Polydorus. That she'd
    give him,
Polymestor, for to keep in trust. Stashed away somewhere. He
    went with her. Yes. He'd give it
To her imp. Her latest son. He would. Then she got him in the
    secret place.
Oh yes. She got him rightly. Oh. Her claws tore out his eyes.
    And then her fingernails
Went in again. Not for his eyes. What eyes? He had no eyes.
    She plucked the dark from out the sockets.

And that was that. She got down on all fours and crawled.
    Shivered her haunches.
Growled. It's over. I have done my time. My time is done.
    What now? What
Will I be? Her jaw distended. Her arms and legs became all
    legs, and claws
Sprang from her toenails. Her bedraggled wiry coat was mired
    with blood.
There was this stone. She ran at it and gnarred at it and
    worried it.
She gawped her mouth to speak, and barked. She tossed the
    stone up
In the air. Her tongue lolled out. She barked and barked again,
    and gowls eternally around the Hellespont.

Contract

Demosthenes climbed the rungs of Larynx, diminuendo in its
    double helix.
He buzzed with words like *gremlin*, *glitch*, *Zeno's Paradox*,
    and *genetrix*.

Sparks and plumbers, carpenters and glaziers vocalized their
    trades' vernacular;
Priests hymned their rounds and hummed and hahhed the
    ropey new funicular.

So this was Brueghel's *Babel*, *Lego*-kit-like Pharaonic phasia-
Bricks, where everything is built in stages, ages, scaffolding,
    and phrases.

An eighth-month unstung tongue was clammed with gummed-
    up syllables
Of forceps: bumble, blunder, umbilicals, and garbled labials.

Then Principalities of angels glided in on wings of myth and
    moth,
Their pockets filled with pebbles; they put the thumby,
    stumbling bees in Plato's mouth.

Bagpipe Music

He came lilting down the brae with a blackthorn stick the thick
  of a shotgun
In his fist, going *blah dithery dump a doodle scattery idle
  fortunoodle* —
When I saw his will-o'-the-wisp go dander through a field of
  blue flax randomly, abandonedly
Till all his dots and dashes zipped together, ripped right
  through their perforations
Like a Zephyr through the Zodiac: the way a quadrille, in its
  last configuration,
Takes on the branches of a swastika, all ribs and shanks and
  male and female chromosomes;
Till I heard his voice diminish like the corncrake's in the last
  abandoned acre —
Scrake tithery lass a laddle nation aries hiber Packie, he'd be

Oblivious to the black-and-tan, leaf-and-muck-bestrewn
  squatting figure
Whose only obvious features are the almost-blue whites of his
  two blue eyes, who crabs
From leaf to shadow, mesmerized by olive and burnt umber,
  the khaki, lion patches
Of his Cockney accent, going *hang bang a bleeper doddle
  doodlebug an asterix.*
The Pisces rod of his aerial twitched just now, as if he'd got the
  message,
That the earth itself was camouflaged. Bluebells carpeted the
  quivered glades, as,
Three fields away, the tick-tock of the grandmother reassures
  us with the long extended
Skillet of its pendulum. The wife in all of this is sidelong,
  poised Egyptian
In her fitted kitchen, though the pictograph is full of *Ireland's
  Own*-type details, Virgin

Marys, blue and white plates ranged like punctuation in the lull
of memory.
The walls are sentences. We see the three walls and the fourth is
glassy us.

Ocularity a moiety blah skiddery ah disparity: the shotgun
made a kind of statement, two
Crows falling in a dead-black umlaut. *The Lucky Shot*, my
man would say, and feed
Me yet another yarn: how you find a creeper in the
undergrowth and yank,
And a rippled, ripped net shivers through its warp of black-
damp earth aroma.
There's ink embedded in his two eyes blue, like children's
dots. Listen close
Enough, you'll get the blooping of the retting dam, parturient,
as bubbles
Pick and pock a morseway through the stench of rotting flax.
For it seemed
The grandmother produced an alarm-clock from her
psychobabble handbag.

That was at the checkpoint. Meanwhile, the trail was
beginning to leak and waft
Away, but the sniffer dogs persevered in their rendition of
The Fox Chase, lapping
And snuffling up the pepper-black stardust fibrillating on the
paper, till
The interview was thwarted by Aquarius, a blue line on the
map that was
Contemporaneous with its past. *Skirl girn a snaffle birdle
girdle on the griddle howlin* —

Here a squad of black-and-white minstrels wheel in from Stage
Right, or rather, they

Are wearing balaklavas, and it only looks like that, their
    grinning
Toothpaste lips, their rolling whites of eyes, their *Tipp-Ex*ed
    teeth, their *Daz* forensic
Gloves. They twirl their walking-sticks as thick as guns to
    marching tunes
That blatter in that fourth green field across the border,
    upstairs in a tent,
With Capricorn-skin drums and fifes, while Blavatsky hollers
    through a bullhorn,
*Give ye thirty shillins for yer wan poun ten, yer wan poun ten,
    yer*
Fair exchange, they say, sure six of one and half-a-dozen of the
    brother —
I get the drift of the *Bloo* in the portable loo, John, like, it's one
    ping cancels out
The pong, going *January, February, March! April, May, June,
    July!*

He was blabbing with his Jew-or-jaw's harp finger on his
    lower lip, when the breech
Of the gun snapped out its breach of the peace. The linen
    handkerchief had got
A brack in it, somehow, the dots and dashes of some other's
    red. I tried to pin it down
Just then, or pen it down, but the Lambegs wouldn't let me,
    and anyway, my thumb
And finger's smeared up to the wrist with *Lion* ink. My hand
    is dis-
Located. The unmarked car came quietly, enquiringly, while
    in a no-go zone
Three streets away, I heard two taxis crabbing, like Gemini in
    Gethsemane, which
Of them was black: *honk parp a bullet billet reverup and harp
    a ballad*

Scrake nithery lou a mackie nice wee neice ah libralassie . . .
Just before I put the thing to bed, I closed a pair of scorpion's
   inverted commas round it.
Tomorrow I would glance at the decapitated headlines, then
   flick forward to the Stars.

58

They'd rehearsed the usual Heinz variety of condoms, clocks,
    fertilizer, and electrical flex,
Plus a Joker's device which, someone claimed, had devolved
    from one of the '50s *Batman* serial flicks —
Which proves there's nothing new *sub specie aeternitatis*, or
    it's part of the general, Heraclitean flux.

Like the orange-sized plastic tomato that glows on the Formica
    counter of the all-night caff,
Your actual's slantindicular as the letter zed, and a long shot
    from being all kiff,
As you'd guess from the blobs and squiggles they'd squidged
    on their chips and someone got on his cuff.

It was raining on the neon writing as they upped and offed and
    packed themselves into the pick-up truck;
The drizzly sound of the words seeped out and will-o'-the-
    wisped on the nearby railway track;
But when the deal came down and the *Enterprise* glimmed
    through, they'd be *n* cards short of a trick.

For they couldn't computate how many beans made five; a
    has-been Celticamerad had vizzed them to the Picts.
And, chauffed through the dark, they were well on the drag to
    becoming commemorative plaques —
Which is hickery-pickery, Indian smoke to the pipe of the
    aberkayheybo Hibernian Pax.

So it's mercury tilt and quicksilver flash as the Johnson
    slammed on the brakes
And it's indecipherababble bits and bods, skuddicked and
    scrabbled like alphabet bricks —
A red hand. A rubber glove. The skewed grin of the clock. A
    clip of ammunition. A breastpocketful of *Bics*.

Ark of the Covenant

1

They palmed it in and hid it in a bog, invisibly, between the
    Islands of Carnmoon
And Island Carragh South: a strange device, concocted from
    the inner workings
Of a fertilizer bag and someone's fertile brain — gyres and
    gimbals, wires and moans.

A vulgate apologia was on the cards already, the orchestra of
    palms upturned and weighed.
It would be interpreted, dismantled, in iodine ablutions of
    The News
Which comes before The Weather: thunderclouds that move in
    symphonies of woad.

Soldiers painted like the palm-and-finger paintings of a child,
    smears of black
Which underline their eyes like eyebrows, so's the light
    won't blind them: they are
Egyptian, mummified and profiled in the *ignis fatuus* of check
    and road-block.

Scrawled hieroglyphs elaborate the black slick of the road.
    Witnesses
Are called upon, but the ink has lightened into amethyst, and
    soon its blue will be
Invisible, as new ideas dawn across the moss. A great
    Panjandrum will construe their Whatnesses.

2

They trojan-horsed it in and stashed it in a bog, intentionally,
    between the Islands of Carnmoon
And Island Carragh South: a palpable device to suit the
    nomothetic military,
Their *sotto voce* blacks and tans; to second-guess the language
    of their brief campaign.

They read it in the Vulgate, words which spoke with high
    authority of semaphore
And palms. And psalms were evident in thunderclouds as
    pyramidal rays of light
Engraved in blue-ish tints, when God's eye glitters through the
    cloudy hemisphere.

He is painted like a waterfall or thundercloud of beard and
    ikon, topaz
Frown that condescends to Bethlehem, where shepherds
    watch by night across
Carnmoon, hunched carmine in the lanternlight, as they
    rehearse the day's momentous topics.

They are the witnesses of snowflake-lazy galaxies, who
    prophesy the moon,
Blue moon that indicates a Second Coming is at hand. It is a
    trip that might be
Wired or not, a trap of wired-up jaws from which ensues the
    vulgate moan.

3

They hushed it in, in its impenetrable black: a bag, a coalsack
    isolated in Carnmoon.
It seethed with good intentions of its maker, trickling
    microseconds slow
As syllables which tick their clock as condensation drips in
    mushroom mines.

The dead black Vulgate of its text is barbed and gothic, and is
    inspired by Yahweh.
Its circuits have been dipped in the blackletter font. They have
    named it *Proclamation*.
And whosoever does not take the word on board will be
    forever called Yahoo

Who are doodled like the antlered stags and men in glyptic
    caves, ritual ochre
Hands imprinted there. The rubric of discarded bones has
    made it difficult to tell
Humerus from humus, as the sheep enact a huddled parliament
    on Carnmoon's snowy acre.

The animals were nodding witnesses, plumes of breath
    illuminated by the birth,
The icy straw. The frankincense and myrhh have taken on a
    cordite odour;
The movable star is relegated to the black bag, where it weeps
    amidst the weeping broth.

4

They'd bound it in a mock book buried in the bog between
    the Islands of Carnmoon
And Island Carragh South, and sniffed the glue and ichor of its
    perfect binding
And its veins. The dope-black seeds of its brain they wrapped
    in husk of cardamom.

Black Vulgate barbs and verbs were conjugated there with
    wired-up quips,
Hosannahs subjugated by the nomothetic tablature. It's
    writhing into future
Tense just now, elaborated by its wish to be, to match the pro
    quos to the quids.

Soldiers, camouflaged as hedges in the hedgeless bog, flit
    through the Islands of Carnmoon.
Their palms are blacked as if for fingerprinting, and the blue
    whites of their eyes
Illuminate the rubric of their Yellow Cards. They slant
    Egyptianly with dog and carbine.

One dog was witness, moaning through the scattered codices
    and hieroglyphs.
The alphabet of troops was learned by rote and entombed in
    the black aplomb
Of a police notebook: an abecedary sans eyes, sans teeth, sans
    everything, and sans serifs.

Ovid: *Metamorphoses*, XIII, 576-619

When Aurora heard about the fate of Hecuba, she didn't care.
She'd troubles of her own. Her own son Memnon, transfixed
    by Achilles'
Spear. He's set upon the pyre. They're going to burn him. She
    offers up a prayer
To Jove: commemorate him in some memorable way. The god
    nods, and says, well, yes.

Memnon's bonfire then collapsed in red and black, the charred
    beams hissed and flickered.
Greasy-thick smoke sputtered up and smutched Aurora's
Sky of rose and pearl. Soot and cinders flocked together in a
    bird-shaped aura
That becomes a bird. Like an opening fist, it creaks its wings.
    Squawks and flutters.

And then the squab engendered other birds innumerable. They
    wheeled
In pyrotechnics round the pyre. The Stukas, on the third
    approach, split
In two like Prods and Taigs. Scrabbed and pecked at one
    another. Sootflecks. Whirl-
Wind. Celtic loops and spirals chawed each other, fell down
    dead and splayed.

And every year from then to this, the Remember Memnon
    birds come back to re-enact
Their civil war. They revel in it, burning out each other. And
    that's a fact.

Opus Operandi

1

Fatima handed out twelve teaching modules of the 'empathy
     belly'
To the variously expectant fathers. Some were Paddy, and
     some were Billy.

Today's lesson was the concept 'Orange'. They parsed it into
     segments: some were kith,
And some were kin. They spat out the pips and learned to peel
     the pith.

Then the deep grammar of the handshake, the shibboleths of
     aitch and *haitch*:
It's a bit like tying knots, whether Gordian or sheepshank,
     clove or hitch.

In the half-dark of their lapidary parliament, you can just make
     out the shape
Of chimeras and minotaurs. Anthropomorphic goats are
     blethering to the demi-sheep.

It seems the gene-pool got contaminated. Everything was
     neither one thing nor the other;
So now they're trying to agree on a formula for a petition to the
     Author.

He's working overtime just now, dismembering a goose for
     goose-quills.
Tomorrow will be calfskin parchment, then the limitation
     clauses and the codicils.

2

Jerome imagined Babel with its laminates and overlapping tongues
And grooves, the secret theatre with its clamps and vices, pincers, tongs.

It's like an Ark or quinquereme he prised apart, to find the little oarsmen
At their benches. They looked somewhat surprised as he began the seminar

On hieroglyphs, using them as prime examples. They began to strain
Against the shackles of his language, his sentences, his full-stop and his chain.

He tapped the clinker-built antique and it disgorged its clichés.
He upturned it and it struggled like a turtle full of cogs and helices.

A school of clocks swarmed out from the Underwood's overturned undercarriage,
Full of alphabetical intentions, led astray by braggadocio and verbiage.

Typecast letters seethed on the carpet, trying to adopt its garbled Turkish
Convolutions. They were baffled by the script's *auctoritas*.

Bug-like, they attached themselves to the underside of the rug and hung there
Bat-like, colonised in non-pareils and minions, hugger-mugger.

3

Dr Moreau contemplated the Doormouse. It was wearing an
    elegant penguin
Suit. Moreau handed it his hat and went on in. He hoped the
    operetta would be sanguine.

Die Fledermaus was dressed up in his usual bat-suit.
    Crocodile-
Skin shoes. A cape for wings, and an absolutely Dracula-like

Dicky-bow. An as-yet-unbloodied bib. He bared his fangs as
    far back as the epiglottis
And began to aria an echolalia of aspirates and glottal stops.

Eventually he found a disguised Countess, and sunk an umlaut
    in her jugular.
He gargled in her tautonyms and phonemes, her Transyl-
    vanian corpuscular.

Her eyes drooled and grew as he imbibed her, as they glided
    through the mirror
And came out on the other side; then, clinging to each other,
    dimmed into tomorrow.

Moreau's yesterday was their tomorrow. His fossil study of
    the pterodactyl
Had led him to believe that man could fly, fuelled by iambics,
    alcohol, and dactyls.

Jerome drank the vision in. He put on his airman's snorkel
    and got into the bubble.
He gave the thumbs-up sign, and set the ultrasonic scan for
    Babel.

In his amphibian, the hero limped home in a grand Byronic Gesture; Fatima dismissed the Twelve; it was the end of therapy and embryonics.

Tak, Tak

for Piotr Sommer

It was on a crackly line from Sulejówek that I learned these first
    few words of Polish,
Meaning *Yes, Of course,* or *Is that so?* The static made me think
    perhaps a Police

Tap. It put me in mind of the Queen's own brand of blotting-
    paper, which is black,
So nobody can read the mirror image of Her private
    correspondence. *Tak?*

Black line, impenetrable-bakelite-black phone: viridian-
    beetle-black, the *tak, tak, tak*
As someone lifted or abandoned a receiver. He clicked the
    snooker cue into the rack;

Or *verbatim,* Vulgate-black like the inside of an unopened
    Bible —
Cessaverunt aedificare civitatem. Et idcirco vocatum est ejus
    Babel.

And in the bas-relief of Babel, serried regiments of Babylonian
    lions blink lazily
From lion-coloured tiles, imprinted on a ground of lapis lazuli.

The antique roar is deep-embedded, throttled in the Leo
    syrinx,
Eroded through with sand and microscopic bits of Sphinx.

Marduk brandished his articulated scorpion-tail.
    Nebuchadnezzar joined Him in the lapis monastery.
Blue glaze of tiles gazed round them, as they re-interpreted
    the Mystery.

They went from *A* to *B* by way of Zed, as far as they could
    figure it,
Which caused their ruination; they became a nation of
    abandoned ziggurats.

And it was on a crackly line from Sulejówek that I learned these
    lines of Polish,
Scrawled by Someone's moving finger in the urinously
    monumental palace —

Ceramic blue and white, glazed over by the whisperings of
    cisterns. It was underground,
Suddenly invaded by the *furioso*, off-course *tak, tak, tak* of
    trains relinquishing The Underground.

Latitude 38° S

1

Then they told the story of the satyr, who played the flute so
    brilliantly
In Phrygia, he tried to beat Apollo. Apollo won, of course; for
    extra measure, thought
He'd bring the satyr down another peg or two: stripped off
    his pelt, ungloving it from

Scalpwards down. And could he play then? With his fingertips
    all raw,
His everything all peeled and skinless? You saw the score of
    veins
Externalized, the palpitating circuits. The polythene-like
    arteries. The pulsing bag
Of guts you'd think might play a tune, if you could bring
    yourself to blow and squeeze it.

2

I flipped the tissue-paper and took in the Christian icon-
    ography.
Its daguerrotype-like, braille feel. The spiky instruments. The
    pincers.
The man who'd invented the saw had studied the anatomy
    of a
Fish's spine. From bronze he cut the teeth and tried them out
    on a boxwood tree.

That ancient boxwood flute of Greece will haunt him yet.
    Through olive groves
Its purple aura bleats through dark and sheep. The dozing
    shepherd

With his flute abandoned. Wrapped up in his mantle,
   independent, fast asleep.

3

I felt like the raw blob of a baby kangaroo that crawls the vertical
Fur of its mother, and falls eventually into the pouch,
   exhaustedly.
As Daedalus was herring-boning feathers into wings, I was
The sticky, thumby wax with which he oozed the quills
   together.

I dropped my red blob on the letter-flap and sunk my
   suddenly-embodied
Thumb in it. The message inside was the obverse harp on an
   Irish ha'penny;
Bronze, unstrummable. It was there for someone else to flip.

4

Fletcher cut the nib of a quill with a Stanley knife and sliced
   the palp
Of his finger off. It quivered with its hinge of skin, then
   rivuletted
On the parchment. He didn't know where it was going. It
   obscured
The nice calligraphy that looked definitive: like a Proclamation
   or a Treaty.

In fact, he'd been trying to copy the *Inquit* page off the Book
Of Kells, as if it were a series of 'unquotes'. The way you'd
   disengage
The lashes of a feather, then try and put them back together.

5

The place was packed with expectant academics, but my
    marking slips
Had flittered away from the text. They'd been *Rizla* papers in
    another
Incarnation, when I'd rolled a smoke between my thumbs and
    fingers, teasing
Out the strands. I waffled on about the stet-detectors in the
    library

Basement, security requirements, conduits, wiring, laminates,
    and ducts.
Up above, the floors and stacks and filing systems, the
    elaborate
Machinery of books, where I materialized. I strummed their
    rigid spiny gamut.

6

There's a shelf of *Metamorphoses*. Commentaries. Lives. *The
    Mystery of Ovid's
Exile.* This is where the Phrygian mode returns, by way of an
    Australian stamp
That's slipped out from the covers, bearing the unlikely-
    looking lyre-shaped
Tail of the lyrebird. Printed in intaglio, it's playing a barcarole.

I think of it as clinker-built, Æolian, floating down the limpid
    river which —
Said Ovid's people — sprang from all the tears the country
    fauns and nymphs
And shepherds wept in Phrygia, as they mourned their friend
    the fettered satyr.

7

So they tell their stories, of the cruelty of gods and words and
    music.
The fledglings of the lyrebird's song. Its arrows. They stare
    into
The water — 'clearest in that Realme' — and see the fishes
    shingled,

Shivered, scalloped on the pebbles. The arrows of the wind
    upon the water,
Written on the water; rolled like smoke, the fluted breath that
    strolls
At midnight. They gaze into the stream's cold pastoral, seeing
Fossil ribs and saws embedded there, the fluteplayer's
    outstretched fingers.

The Albatross

After Baudelaire, L'Albatros

Often, for a gag, the Jack Tars like to catch an albatross, Aviator
Of the high seas, who, following the navy, wants to be its
    Avatar.

But they slap him, Emperor of Blue, down on the salty planks.
    They taunt him.
Spat at, tripped up, his wings creak helplessly like oars, and
    haunt him.

This wingèd voyager, now bedraggled, ugly, awkward, how
    pathetic!
Someone pokes a pipe into his mouth, and someone else who
    mimics him is paralytic.

The Poet's like that Prince of Clouds, who soars above the
    archer and the hurricane: Great Auk
Brought down to earth, his gawky, gorgeous wings impede his
    walking.

The Ballad of HMS *Belfast*

On the first of April, *Belfast* disengaged her moorings, and
    sailed away
From old Belfast. Sealed orders held our destination,
    somewhere in the Briny Say.

Our crew of Jacks was aromatic with tobacco-twist and
    alcoholic
Reekings from the night before. Both Catestants and
    Protholics,

We were tarry-breeked and pig-tailed, and sailed beneath the
    White Ensign;
We loved each other nautically, though most landlubbers
    thought we were insane.

We were full-rigged like the *Beagle*, piston-driven like the
    Enterprise
Express; each system was a back-up for the other, auxiliarizing
    verse with prose.

Our engines ticked and tacked us up the Lough, cranks and
    link-pins, cross-rods
Working ninety to the dozen; our shrouds and ratlines rattled
    like a cross-roads

Dance, while swivels, hook blocks, cleats, and fiddles jigged
    their semi-colons
On the staves. We staggered up the rigging like a bunch of
    demi-golems,

Tipsy still, and dreamed of underdecks — state-rooms, crystal
    chandeliers,
And saloon bars — until we got to gulp the ozone; then we
    swayed like gondoliers

Above the aqua. We gazed at imperceptible horizons, where amethyst
    Dims into blue, and pondered them again that night, before the mast.

Some sang of Zanzibar and Montalban, and others of the lands unascertained
    On maps; we entertained the Phoenix and the Unicorn, till we were grogged and concertina'ed.

We've been immersed, since then, in cruises to the Podes and Antipodes;
    The dolphin and the flying fish would chaperone us like aquatic aunties

In their second, mermaid childhood, till we ourselves felt neither fish nor flesh, but
    Breathed through gills of rum and brandy. We'd flounder on the randy decks like halibut.

Then our Captain would emerge to scold us from his three days' incommunicado
    And promenaded on the poop-deck, sashed and epauletted like a grand Mikado

To bribe us with the Future: new Empires, Realms of Gold, and precious ore
    Unheard-of since the days of Homer: we'd boldly go where none had gone before.

Ice to Archangel, tea to China, coals to Tyne: such would be our cargo.
    We'd confound the speculators' markets and their exchequered, logical embargo.

Then were we like the *Nautilus*, that trawls the vast and purple catacomb
For cloudy shipwrecks, settled in their off-the-beam, intractable aplomb.

Electric denizens glide through the Pisan masts, flickering their Pisces' *lumière*;
We regard them with a Cyclops eye, from our bathyscope beneath *la mer*.

Scattered cutlery and dinner-services lie, hugger-mugger, on the murky floor.
An empty deck-chair yawns and undulates its awning like a semaphore.

Our rising bubble then went *bloop, bloop* till it burst the swaying window-pane;
Unfathomed from the cobalt deep, we breathed the broad Pacific once again.

Kon-Tiki-like, we'd drift for days, abandoning ourselves to all the elements,
Guided only by the aromatic coconut, till the wind brought us the scent of lemons —

Then we'd disembark at Vallambroso or Gibraltar to explore the bars;
Adorned in sequin-scales, we glimmered phosphorescently like stars

That crowd innumerably in midnight harbours. O olive-dark interior,
All splashed with salt and wine! Havana gloom within the humidor!

The atmosphere dripped heavy with the oil of anchovies,
   tobacco-smoke, and chaw;
We grew languorous with grass and opium and *kif*, the very
   best of draw,

And sprawled in urinous piazzas; slept until the fog-horn
   trump of Gabriel.
We woke, and rubbed our eyes, half-gargled still with
   braggadocio and garble.

And then the smell of docks and ropeworks. Horse-dung. The
   tolling of the Albert clock.
Its Pisan slant. The whirring of its ratchets. Then everything
   began to click:

I lay bound in iron chains, alone, my *aisling* gone, my sentence
   passed.
Grey Belfast dawn illuminated me, on board the prison ship
   Belfast.

Acknowledgements

Acknowledgements are due to the editors of *element*, *The Honest Ulsterman*, *The Irish Review*, *The Irish Times*, *The London Review of Books*, *Poetry Review*, *Snark*, *Soho Square*, and *The Times Literary Supplement*, where some of these poems were published first.

I am grateful to Michael Hofmann and James Lasdun for guiding me towards Ovid's *Metamorphoses*.